A book
is a present you can open
again and again.

THIS BOOK BELONGS TO

FROM

All About Holidays
with Inspector McQ

Written by Kathleen Kain
Illustrated by Ben Mahan

World Book, Inc.
a Scott Fetzer company
Chicago London Sydney Toronto

Printed in the United States of America
ISBN 0-7166-1628-9
Library of Congress Catalog Card No. 91-65757

8 9 10 11 12 13 14 15 99 98 97 96

Cover design by Rosa Cabrera
Inspector McQ illustrated by Eileen Mueller Neill

Greetings. My name is Inspector McQuestion—McQ for short. If you're like me, you probably wonder about a lot of things. Take the holidays we celebrate each year. Have you ever wondered how they all began? Come along with me, and we'll find out.

Why is New Year's Day on January 1 **?**

Why indeed! Let's travel back a few hundred years to find the answer.

Hundreds of miles away in Europe, it's the 1500's. March marks the beginning of the new year. This makes good sense. Spring arrives in March, and the whole world seems new in spring.

But wait. The calendar is a bit confusing. Every year isn't exactly the same length. The seasons are getting "later" each year, according to the calendar, at least. Farmers certainly can't plant and harvest according to a calendar.

Finally Pope Gregory XIII, the leader of the Catholic Church then, introduced a more exact calendar. This calendar began every year on a certain day, January 1, and ended on a certain day, December 31. That's more organized, don't you think?

The new calendar grew more and more popular over the years, and settlers who came to North America started following it in 1752. We've been celebrating New Year's Day on January 1 ever since.

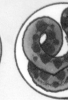

How are the Chinese New Years named?

Boom! I hear firecrackers and the roll of drums. Is that a dragon coming down the street? I'd better stay out of its way! The Chinese New Year parade is coming. What is so special about the Chinese New Year celebration?

Let's go back to China long ago. Each year is said to honor an important part of nature: wood, fire, earth, metal, or water. And each year is named for an animal important to the people's beliefs. According to an old legend, these twelve animals finished a cross-country race in this order: rat, ox, tiger, hare, dragon, snake, horse, sheep, monkey, rooster, dog, and pig. (I'd love to see such a race!) So the new year might become the year of the rat, then the year of the ox, for example.

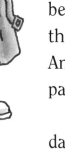

Each traditional Chinese year still is named for one of the animals. The new year begins sometime between January 21 and February 19, according to the position of the new moon at the time. Chinese Americans celebrate the new year holiday with parties and parades.

If I watch out for that dragon, it's a fun, colorful day for me, too!

How did Ground-Hog Day begin?

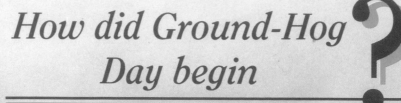

Ground-Hog Day began in England and Germany. Here are the facts.

According to an old belief, February 2 was supposed to be a good day to look for signs of spring. On that day, English farmers waited for a hedgehog or a bear to peek out of its burrow after a long winter sleep. German farmers watched for a badger. If the day was sunny, the animal saw its shadow. Folks thought the animal must be afraid of its shadow and run back into the burrow. There it would sleep for six more weeks, and spring weather would be late.

Now if the day were cloudy, the animal was thought to stay outside. Then the farmers expected an early spring.

German and English settlers in North America switched the animal in the legend to a ground hog because that's the animal they saw more often here. The ground hog has been our unofficial "spring forecaster" ever since. I wonder what the ground hog thinks of all this!

Where did Valentine's Day come from ?

Over 2,000 years ago, people known as Romans used to hold games and dances in the middle of February in honor of one of their many gods. Each boy would draw the name of a girl to be his partner. The couples sometimes became sweethearts.

Time passed, and many Romans adopted the religion of Christianity, rather than believe in many gods. But they didn't give up their February festivities. Instead, they celebrated on a February day that honored a Christian saint named Valentine. (A saint is someone specially honored by the Christian religion.)

Little is known about Saint Valentine. He was a priest and doctor in Rome who died around the year 269. An old story tells how he cured a little girl of blindness. According to the story, he once wrote her a letter and signed it, "from your Valentine." Today, we've gotten away from the Roman-style dances and games on Valentine's Day. But everyone still likes to get cards signed, "from your Valentine"— don't you think?

Who is the Easter Rabbit **?**

A rabbit hopping along with a basket of eggs? How *do* such things get started?

As you may have figured out by now, lots of holidays have to do with changing seasons. Long before Christianity came about, people rejoiced during what is now called Easter time. Budding plants and newborn animals seemed to shout: "It's spring!" The hare—a larger cousin of the rabbit—especially stood for birth and new life. Even today we can see why. A mother hare may have five to six litters a year.

For early people in the country of Egypt, the hare was also a symbol of the moon because it fed at night. And here's another connection between hares and Easter. The moon determines when we celebrate Easter: on the Sunday after the full moon on or after the first day of spring.

A German duchess came up with the story of an Easter hare who laid eggs and hid them for children to find. German settlers in the United States spread the customs of the Easter hare and the egg hunt to the United States. Today this delightful character, known as the Easter Rabbit or Easter Bunny, *brings* goodies. A visit from him is still a sure sign that spring is here.

Why do we have Earth Day

What a day! The sky looks so blue, fresh air tickles my whiskers, a stream ripples nearby, trees sway in the breeze: I love Planet Earth! There's no other place quite like it.

Earth Day celebrates taking care of the earth. It is not a holiday that goes back hundreds of years. It began here in the United States just a little over twenty years ago. Lots of people were concerned about litter, too much garbage, dirty exhaust from cars, polluted rivers—anything that could hurt the earth.

Earth lovers wanted to spread the message: "Keep the earth clean and healthful for people and other living things. Earth is our only home." Earth Day became established on April 22, although communities might vary the date, too.

Earth Day is a day to join your neighbors, friends, and classmates for special earth projects. Yet, if you're like me, every day is Earth Day. Let's get that litter and pack some cans off to the recycling center.

15

Who started Mother's Day and Father's Day?

Both these days started with a special mother and father.

Anna Jarvis grew up in West Virginia, not long after the Civil War ended in 1865. That was a war between the northern and southern states in our country. There was a lot of disagreement in some families because soldiers from the same family might have been on different sides during the war. Anna's mother wished that there was a holiday called Mother's Day. She believed that brothers would make peace with each other on their mother's special day.

When Anna grew up, she carried out her mother's wishes. She spread the idea of Mother's Day, and it became popular. She wrote to world leaders asking them to make Mother's Day an official holiday. In 1914, the President of the United States made the second Sunday in May Mother's Day.

And Father's Day? A lady named Sonora Dodd, inspired by Mother's Day, got the same idea for a father's day. She wanted to honor her own father, who raised his family alone after Sonora's mother had died. Mrs. Dodd spread the idea, and it began to catch on early in the 1900's, just as Mother's Day was doing so. Today it's official: Father's Day is the third Sunday in June.

Anna's mother and Sonora's father were pretty special parents with pretty special children, wouldn't you say?

17

What are two days for parades in May

The weather is getting warmer and I'm getting ready for some parades and outdoor festivities. What's to celebrate in May, I wonder?

Aha! Cinco de Mayo! This is a Spanish term that means "Fifth of May." Back in 1862, Mexican troops won an important battle against French troops who were trying to take over Mexico. Ever since, people in Mexico and many Mexican Americans in the United States have celebrated this proud day with festivals, parades, and parties.

18

And if it's May, Memorial Day must be coming up, too. This is a day of flags, parades, and picnics. What does Memorial Day really mean? To find the answer, we have to go back to the Civil War again.

During this terrible time, many families lost loved ones. They wanted to remember those who died by decorating their graves on a special day. The idea caught on and, as time passed, Memorial Day became a national holiday on the last Monday in May.

Modern Memorial Days seem happy and carefree. Schools close and many families might have barbecues. It's a day to have fun but also a day to remember those who died in war.

Why do we celebrate the Fourth of July ?

Let's look back in history to find out why July 4 is a famous day. Here's the story.

Americans declared their freedom from rule by the British government on July 4, 1776. British lawmakers had been passing laws that hurt American business. They demanded heavy taxes. The British even sent soldiers to make certain that the Americans obeyed the laws and paid the taxes. This was the last straw!

Americans began making plans to break away from the British government. Fighting flared up in towns such as Lexington and Concord in Massachusetts. A group of American leaders, called the Continental Congress, met to decide what to do. The Congress included future presidents John Adams and Thomas Jefferson. Jefferson wrote the Declaration of Independence and it was adopted on July 4, 1776.

Ever since, we have celebrated our country's birthday on July 4. Do you watch fireworks or go to a parade that day? Now you know what it's all for!

What does "Halloween" mean?

That is a mystery, but a good mystery always interests me. The answer took just a little snooping.

Thousands of years ago, a people named the Celts lived in the countries that we call England, Scotland, and Ireland today. Around what is now November 1, the Celts thought that their summer-loving sun god went to war with the god of winter. They believed that the god of winter sent an army of ghosts and goblins along with the cold. So on the night before November 1, the people dressed in animal skins to hide from scary creatures, and they built bonfires to shoo them away.

After hundreds of years the Celts became Christians. November 1 became a Christian holiday called All Saints' Day or All Hallows' Day. (*Hallow* is an old word for "holy.") October 31, or the night before All Hallows' Day, was All Hallows' E'en, which means "evening." Later, All Hallows' E'en was shortened to Halloween. Christians no longer believed in the god of winter. But they still celebrated Halloween with costumes and bonfires.

What does all this prove? Just that Halloween is one of those very old holidays and dressing up and spooky times are still fun.

Why do we have Thanksgiving Day

That's another good question. Early settlers called Pilgrims celebrated the first Thanksgiving in America. One of the Pilgrims, Edward Winslow, left an eyewitness account. It may give us a clue.

Winslow wrote that the Pilgrims had harvested their first crop in America. So they decided to "rejoice together" in a "special manner." Hunters caught enough wild birds to feed the Pilgrims for a week. The American Indians who had fed and helped the Pilgrims for many months joined in the feasting.

Maybe the Pilgrims were homesick. For hundreds of years before the Pilgrims left their homes in England, the English had celebrated their harvests with feasts and games. This celebration was called Harvest Home.

So, in answer to the question—Thanksgiving Day is for rejoicing about a good harvest, and so many other things to be thankful for. I bet you can think of lots of them.

What is Hanukkah

Like many holidays, Hanukkah has a good story behind it. Here's what I found out.

More than 2,000 years ago, a king of a country called Syria ruled Israel, the land of the Jewish people. Since the Syrian king tried to stop the Jews from practicing their religion, five brothers called the Maccabees led a rebellion against the Syrians. Now the king's troops far outnumbered the Jewish rebels. But the Jews still managed to drive the Syrians out of the city of Jerusalem, the home of their temple.

After the Jewish victory, the Maccabees wanted to rededicate their temple to God. First they needed to light the temple menorah, a kind of oil lamp. They had enough oil to burn the lamp for one day. Yet, legend has it that the oil burned for eight days instead of one.

For eight days, usually in December, the Jews celebrate Hanukkah, which means "dedication." Each night Jewish families light a new candle on the menorah. The candles remind them about winning freedom and keeping the temple lamp burning.

Why do people have Christmas trees❓

No mystery here. Most likely, people have Christmas trees because they enjoy the pine scent or the pretty colors and lights.

But where did people get the idea of putting Christmas trees in their homes? It may have come from Rome. Even in the days before Christianity, Romans celebrated their own holiday during what is now Christmastime. They decorated their homes with lights and evergreen branches. Perhaps these gave Christians the idea of decorating trees for Christmas.

Later, people in Germany developed a custom of decorating a Christmas tree in their homes with fruit, nuts, lighted candles and paper flowers. German settlers brought the Christmas tree custom to the United States in the 1800's.

Customs old and customs changing here and there — that's what holidays are all about!

What holiday celebrates African traditions?

It's almost the end of the year, a time to look back and look ahead, too. Kwanzaa is a holiday that does both.

Many African Americans in the United States celebrate Kwanzaa from December 26 to January 1. Kwanzaa celebrates traditional African harvests. In fact, the word *Kwanzaa* comes from a term that means "first fruits" in an African language called Swahili.

Look what a lovely celebration we have here! This family is lighting candles, one new one each day, for the seven days of Kwanzaa. The straw mats and the ears of corn remind the celebrators of African traditions. But Kwanzaa is a holiday that helps people look forward to working together for a good future, too. On the last day, several families may gather together for a special feast with music and dancing—called a *karamu*. A perfect way to end a holiday, and start another year!

We've certainly covered a lot of holiday ground. But we've found some good answers, don't you think? Until next time, this is Inspector McQ, saying, "Keep those questions. I'll find answers for you in my next book."

To Parents

Children love to ask questions. *All About Holidays*, with special mouse detective McQ, will provide your child with the answers to many common questions children ask about holidays. These answers will serve as a bridge into learning some important concepts. Here are a few easy and natural ways your child can express feelings and understandings about what Inspector McQ has to say. You know your child and can best judge which ideas she or he will enjoy most.

You and your child might enjoy making a holiday collage. Think of things that go with different holidays—Thanksgiving turkey, Valentine heart, Halloween pumpkin, Fourth of July flag. On colored posterboard, draw or cut out and paste pictures of holiday symbols to make your collage.

Children like making things to give to others. Suggest that you and your child use construction paper and other materials to make greeting cards for family and friends for an upcoming holiday.

A good way to keep up with the holidays is to use a calendar. Help your child make a calendar for the year. Draw and number a set of boxes representing the days of the months on 12 sheets of paper. Decorate the page for each month with a suitable picture. Add the holidays named in the book. Then add birthdays, anniversaries, or other special days.

Play a holiday memory game. Cut out 12 or more 1½-inch squares of heavy paper or cardboard. Have your child draw holiday symbols, for example, Thanksgiving Pilgrim hats on two squares, menorahs for Hanukkah on two more, Easter eggs on two more, and so on. When you have 12–16 cards, place them face down in three or four rows and take turns trying to uncover matched cards, remembering more pictures as the game proceeds.

Make a holiday family poster with your child. On a large piece of construction paper, he or she can trace an outline of each family member's hand. Then family members can write something about the particular holiday on each finger of their hand outline. For example, on a Thanksgiving poster, have everyone write things they are thankful for; on a Christmas poster, things they would like for Christmas; and on a New Year's poster, resolutions. Decorate the poster with holiday symbols.